THE MINISTRY OF HOSPITALITY

Msgr. James A. Comiskey

THE LITURGICAL PRESS
Collegeville, Minnesota 56321

*To the people of
Christ the King Cathedral Parish
in whom I find Christ.*

Cover design by Ann Blattner. Photo by James L. Shaffer.

Copyright © 1989 by The Order of St. Benedict, Inc., Collegeville, Minnesota. All rights reserved. Printed in the United States of America. ISBN 0-8146-1812-X.

CONTENTS

Introduction		5
Chapter 1	Hospitality: Our Roots and Traditions	7
2	Hospitality: Signs and Earmarks	13
3	Sacramental Moments: Sunday Liturgy	18
4	Sacramental Moments: First Eucharist	20
5	Sacramental Moments: First Reconciliation	23
6	Teaching	25
7	Serving	29
8	Greeting	32
9	Day by Day	34
Conclusion		36
References		37
Litany of Hospitality		38
Examination of Conscience for a Member of the Assembly		39
Baptismal Follow-up Letter		40

The author, Msgr. James A. Comiskey, welcomes a family to a liturgy at Christ the King Cathedral, Lubbock, Texas.

Photo by Jeff Koym. Used with permission.

Introduction

This booklet began with prayer and reflection as I worked on the preparation of a Sunday homily. The readings for that weekend seemed to contain the idea of hospitality. Throughout the week I began to reflect on the ways in which our parish faith community either shows hospitality or hopes and dreams of areas where we might share hospitality better. In reflection, it seemed to me that the spirit of hospitality that is present in our parish results from the ongoing dialogue of many people sharing with me their dream and vision of what our parish could be and of my sharing my vision and dream with them. Hospitality in our parish did not develop overnight; it has evolved over the years. We are aware that we still have a long way to go.

The theme of the January 1988 study week of the Southwest Liturgical Conference held in Corpus Christi, Texas, was "The Assembly, Becoming One Body." The next stage of the booklet was a response to an invitation from Sr. Jeremy Gallet, the local chairperson of the study week, to lead a workshop at the Conference on "Hospitality in the Parish." Sister Jeremy wanted a pastor to address this theme. She suggested that the workshop explore the place of hospitality in the parish in a general way and also share ideas of how hospitality might be fostered at Eucharist. She emphasized "the practical."

Following the workshop in Corpus Christi, I was invited

to expand the workshop material for publication. This booklet on the ministry of hospitality is the result.

As pastor, I try to encourage and animate the members of our parish and also urge them to share their talents with others beyond our parish. With this in mind, I invited Sherry Bitsche and Dena Gonzales to work with me on the workshop presentation. At that time Sherry Bitsche was teaching sixth, seventh, and eighth grade religion in our middle school. She was also one of the cantors for Sunday liturgy. She has a special talent for preparing liturgies for children. Dena Gonzales is in charge of environment in our cathedral. She is a lector and Eucharistic minister. Both of them have assisted in the preparation of parish and diocesan liturgical celebrations. At the back of this booklet there is an examination of conscience that Sherry prepared, and there is a litany of hospitality that Dena prepared. I wish there were some way that I could further share with you their lively and charming contributions.

The song says "I get by with a little help from my friends." In my case, it runs more like "I survive with a lot of help from my friends." My thanks to Margaret Andrews, Emily Severe, and Pat Leach. They were the ones who did the work on the typewriter and the word processor. My gratitude to Myra Morgan, our pastoral assistant, and Virginia Cirone, a former teacher of English in our school. These friends made corrections and gave helpful suggestions.

As you read this booklet, you will note that there are hundreds of talented people involved in the work of our parish faith community. They are loving, caring, hospitable people. They make the booklet a living document.

1

Hospitality: Our Roots and Traditions

Hospitality has been part of our Judeo-Christian tradition from the beginning. Fr. John McKenzie in his *Dictionary of the Bible*[1] points out that desert hospitality was a necessity for survival, and since this necessity fell upon all alike, any guest was entitled to hospitality from any host. Should host and guest be at enmity, the acceptance of hospitality involved a reconciliation. The guest, once accepted by the host, was sacred and must be protected from any danger, even at the cost of the life of family members. In the Jewish Scriptures (Gen 18:1-5), we find Abraham entertaining angels and offering them special hospitality:

> The Lord appeared to Abraham by the terebinths of Mamre. As Abraham was sitting at the opening of his tent in the heat of the day, he looked up and saw three men standing in front of him. When he saw them, he ran from the opening of his tent to meet them and bowed low to the ground. "Sirs," he said, "if I have deserved your favor, do not pass by my humble self without a visit. Let me send for some water so that you may wash your feet and rest under a tree; and let me fetch a little food so that you may refresh yourselves. Afterwards you may continue the journey which has brought you my way." They said, "Do by all means as you say."

A part of hospitality is the desire to reach out—"Let me help." Tied to that desire is your gracious acquiescence—"Do, by all means."

Our old friend Job, in speaking his defense against the accusations of his three friends, reminds them that whenever he saw the wanderer or the poor person without clothing, he warmed them with sheepskin, and he tells of his hospitality to the stranger and the wayfarer, noting, "No stranger lodged in the street if I knew it" (31:32).

In the Second Book of Kings (4:8 ff.) we find a lovely story of hospitality. Elisha, the holy man of God, makes friends with a couple in a certain town. Every time he comes to the town, the couple offers him hospitality in the form of meals. After this happens several times, the woman decides that they can arrange a place in the house for the holy man to stay. Elisha asks his friend and servant if there is anything they can do for the couple. Elisha's friend, Gehazi, points out that the couple has no son. The action of hospitality on the part of the couple is rewarded by the promise of a son.

If you ask people to name their favorite psalm, for many of them The Good Shepherd psalm (Ps 23) wins hands down. In that psalm our God offers us hospitality. We remind God in gratitude: "You set the table before me in the sight of my foes. You anoint my head with oil . . . you make my cup overflow." How delightful to share the hospitality of our God!

Among our least favorite people in the Scriptures are the Bethlehem dwellers who can "find no room for them in the inn" (Luke 2:7). How many homilists have dwelt on this bit of inhospitality down through the years!

Jesus is a person of his times. As he reminds us, he comes "eating and drinking and is a scandal." In Luke's Gospel (7:36 ff.), Jesus goes to the house of Simon. An unnamed woman enters, cries over his reclining body, dries his feet with her hair, and perfumes them with oil. The good host Simon is scandalized. Jesus responds to Simon's thought. "Friend Simon . . . I was an invited guest . . . but . . . you gave me no water for my feet . . . you gave me no kiss . . . you did not anoint my head with oil." Jesus chides Simon for his lack of hospitality. The punch line is almost like the lesson of a parable. "Little is forgiven to one whose love is small." I don't know about you, but I find the gentleness and patience and care of Jesus in this scene unbelievable in its tenderness.

If you page through the Acts of the Apostles, you find many instances where Paul and his companions are offered hospitality along the way in the form of short or long visits in homes, shared meals, and in general, good company while the Word of the Lord is being shared.

When Paul writes to the Romans, he urges them to look on the needs of the saints as their own: "Be generous in your hospitality" (12:13).

The author of the letters to Timothy and Titus is concerned that bishops be hospitable people. The First Letter of Paul to Timothy states, "A bishop should be married once, of even temper, and hospitable" (3:2). In the Letter of Paul to Titus, the bishop should be "hospitable and a lover of goodness" (1:8).

Jesus likens the one who has heard his words and put them into practice to the man who, when he was building his house, dug deep and put the house on a foundation of rock (Matt 25:3 ff.).

Is there a Jesus foundation on which we can build our thinking about hospitality? Surely there is.

I would like to propose that the base or center of the ministry of Christian hospitality is the service of one to another. In serving and being served, at whatever level, I find Christ there, totally hosting and operating in my life and in the lives of the people in a Christian community.

When does Jesus give us such a foundation? How does he teach us this lesson?

In John's Gospel (15:1 ff.), Jesus gives his beautiful and powerful teaching on the relationship that exists between himself and us, and as a consequence, the relationship of each of us to the other. Jesus tells us that a life-giving, life-sustaining relationship is possible with his Father as the vinegrower, with him as the stock of the vine, and with each of us as the branches. The fruit resulting from this fortuitous joining results in good works. It all sounds so simple. Yet as we think it through, we begin to understand the powerful implications of what he is saying. How close would he be to each of us? So close that he is not just *with* us but *in* us. *In us* in terms of a life relationship. If Jesus and I are one in this life relationship, and Jesus and you are one in this life relationship, then think what that says to each of us about the other. How *do* I treat you? How *must* I treat you? Jesus speaks of the joy, the love, and the willingness to do for one another even to the point of giving one's life. I *must* extend hospitality to the other person who shares such a relationship in Christ with me!

Matthew 25:31ff. has a marvelous scene in which Jesus describes the last judgment. How will it happen? The Son of Man will assemble all the nations. When they are assembled, they will be divided into two groups, one to the left and one to the right. Then Jesus spells out the criteria for judging. If he had invited our opinion, what kind of list would we have given him? The list that we use when we examine our conscience? A list of the commandments of the Church? The Son of Man spells out his way of making judgment. What is the key point? Always it is a form of service to another, whether it is to the hungry, the thirsty, the naked, the prisoner, the stranger, or the ill. The point in each case is that we are to find *him* in our brothers and sisters. For having done "whatever it is" for the least of our brothers and sisters, we have done it for Jesus. We find *him* there. We extend hospitality in *his* name.

St. Paul can but echo the same. Blinded on the road to Damascus, he discovers that Christ wills to identify with each person who believes in his name (Acts 26:12ff.). Later, St. Paul will try over and over to tell us of our Christ-unity by using a comparison. The comparison that he uses builds on a story that almost every person in Paul's Greco-Roman world would have known. It is based on one of Aesop's fables:

> The Stomach and the Members
> One fine day it occurred to the members of the body that they were doing all the work while the stomach was getting all the food. So they held a meeting, and after a long discussion, decided to strike until the stomach should take its proper share of the work. So for a day or two, the hands refused to take the food, the mouth refused to receive it, and the teeth had no work to do. After a day or two, the members began to find that they themselves were not in a very active condition. The hands could hardly move, the mouth was all parched and dry, while the legs were unable to support the rest. Thus they found that even the stomach in its dumb, quiet way was doing necessary work for the body and that all parts must work together or the whole body would suffer.[2]

The Romans would have seen this as a story of people and their relationships within the state. But St. Paul recasts the story. In so doing, he spells out for us our relationship with Christ within his new body and our relationships within that body. He uses a living entity. A body! Alive! One part is not able to truly function without the other. It is vine and branches all over again.

In the Gospel of St. Luke, 24:13ff., we find two disciples on the road to Emmaus. It is Sunday night and they, with heavy hearts, have left the city of Jerusalem. As they walk and talk, they are joined by a stranger. They tell the stranger how they had hoped that Jesus of Nazareth might be the Messiah. They tell how the leaders of the people had tried Jesus and crucified him. They tell how some of the women claimed three days later to have seen him alive. The stranger then begins to talk with them. He explains the Jewish prophecies that refer to the Messiah and how they tie in with Jesus. When they get to the town, the two offer the stranger hospitality. He accepts and eats with them. During the meal they recognize Jesus in the breaking of the bread. What a powerful way to reward hospitality!

Abraham, our father in faith, extends hospitality to strangers only to discover that, unknowingly, he has entertained angels. The two thousand years of our history as Roman Catholic Christians are filled with stories of people who offered hospitality to the stranger or to the beggar or to the child or to the leper, only to discover that the person to whom they offered the action of hospitality was the Lord. Martin of Tours shares half his cloak with the *beggar*. *No*, with the Christ. Francis of Assisi kisses the *leper*. *No*, he kisses the Christ. St. Benedict in his *Rule* says, "Be kind to the stranger or the pilgrim." Every visitor is to be treated as if he were Christ.

2

Hospitality: Signs and Earmarks

Fr. Jim Dunning of the North American Forum on the Catechumenate tells a story about himself. It seems that he and a priest friend, Fr. Ray Kemp, found themselves in San Diego on a weekend. A local priest directed them to a particular Catholic church, but they had to park about a block away. As they neared the church, they noticed pairs of teenagers stationed on the sidewalk. As they approached, the teenagers asked if they were going to Mass. An affirmative response brought a welcome complete with an exchange of names, initiated by the young people. As they walked up the steps of the church, there were two women stationed about halfway, and again they were welcomed and names were exchanged. When they entered the church, two men came forward, and the process was repeated. An usher introduced himself and led them down the aisle. When they entered the pew, the people in the pew stood up and introduced themselves. So by the time they began some private prayer before Mass, they had been extended hospitality by about ten people. They happened to visit the church on a Sunday when the Gospel dealt with Jesus calling people to service. The pastor, after the homily, began to call forward the people in the congregation who were involved in service. Finally, the entire sanctuary and front part of the church was filled with members of the congregation. The only people left in the pews were visitors. Before the group returned to their places, all of the visitors (who by then no longer felt like visitors) were invited to stand, and the group in the front applauded them. The two priests agreed that they had seldom felt so much at home.

The ministry of hospitality permeates the whole of parish life. A worshiping community is conscious of hospitality and will do everything possible to make even the exterior of the worship building inviting. Where possible, lawns, trees, shrubs, and flowers must invite. Sloped curbing and special parking places for those who are elderly or handicapped speak of our desire to have them be part of the community. Ramps from car door to church entrance can be important. When we noted in our parish bulletin that it would be helpful to have a wheelchair available, a generous person provided the parish with one.

All too often, the inside gathering spaces of our church buildings, large or small, are not conducive to hospitality. These spaces are frequently dark and colorless or plastered with posters of various kinds and are just not inviting. Entrance space *can* be carefully planned. Many new churches have sufficient gathering space with carpet, living plants, small trees, paintings, even comfortable chairs that can make the first impression warm and hospitable.

What a delightful idea it is for the parish in San Diego not only to have people meet and greet at the door but to meet and greet people outside the church as well! While that might not work in mid-January in Maine or Minnesota as well as it does in San Diego, greeting people at church is a beautiful way in which to begin the ministry of hospitality.

Because we all want to feel at home, having someone meet us, smile at us, reach out a hand, and say a word of greeting usually puts us at our ease. Many times the business world is better at those amenities than the church world. Jesus comments on this in the Scriptures (Luke 16:8). We have a greeter at most of our banks in town, the restaurant usually has the host seat you, the flight attendant meets you as you board the plane, and still another waits inside the airport with information as you leave. The business world knows that hospitality pays important dividends and often does a better job of utilizing God-given talents than we do in our parish communities.

Every time we have some sort of diocesan function in our cathedral, we involve people in the ministry of hospitality as greeters. The ideal people to extend hospitality are the ushers. If they can be persuaded to be ministers of hospitality, that is an excellent way to go. If they are reluctant for whatever reason, then others could exercise this ministry. We have two to four people at each entrance of the cathedral building. They are identified with a badge and ribbons in red and white, which are the cathedral colors. Unless the weather does not permit, there are still other greeters standing at the back of the parking lot. These greeters are able to direct the clergy (deacons and priests) to the place where they will vest. They are also able to assist people who may be bringing food or other items that will be part of a reception or gathering following the cathedral event. Inside the building where the clergy vest, helpful persons provide directions and beverages while waiting for the procession to form.

Many Eucharistic presiders find that another measure of hospitality, as well as a community builder, is to invite all of those present to introduce themselves to the persons around them. An appropriate time for this could be as the commentator or lector approaches the microphone to briefly greet the people and to announce the name of the presiding priest. This could also be done either by the deacon or by the priest-presider after the opening hymn and before he invites all present to make the Sign of the Cross with him.

A number of priests have remarked on the almost tangible difference in the gathered assembly after they have made such a greeting and invitation. There is more packed into this greeting than just names exchanged. There seems to be the sense that *yes, both of us are here to worship the Lord on this Lord's Day. Yes, both of us are believers in Christ the Lord.* Perhaps even the further sense of *yes, we share a unity because both of us are one in Christ.* Maybe everyone would not articulate it in exactly that manner, but that kind of feeling is there after such an exchange on a Sunday morning as worship begins.

A number of parishes try to keep the idea of hospitality before people by reminding members of the parish to stop long enough at the end of Mass to visit awhile with the people they met during Mass. Short reminders in the bulletin from time to time keep the idea of hospitality in the forefront as a ministry for the whole parish. A kind of bonus can develop from this if people follow through on the suggestion. Instead of leaving after Communion or at some other moment before the final hymn is completed, people want to stay and visit with friends who regularly celebrate at "their Mass" on Sunday.

Parishes from one end of our country to the other schedule some sort of after-Mass time to allow people to come together. There is a parish in San Antonio (to single out one) that has involved the different parish organizations within the parish. On one Sunday the Women's Organization members are the greeters at the beginning and end of Mass, and also they are in charge of doughnuts and coffee in the parish hall. The Sunday duties are rotated among each group—the Knights of Columbus, Home and School Association, the C.Y.O. and so forth. Not only are these groups meeting the members of the parish as well as the visitors but also the parish members are meeting different service groups while experiencing moments of hospitality.

You can talk to any number of pastors from rural parishes whose communities serve a meal or part of a meal after the Masses. Such gatherings make for hospitality, build community, and are fund-raisers for the organizations involved. In some parts of the country, they claim that bingo "built our school." In Texas, they claim that sausage suppers or tacos and enchiladas built the church and keep it going.

More to the point, wouldn't it be great if each of our Catholic churches were known and recognized as that friendly church in the community!

3

Sacramental Moments: Sunday Liturgy

A part of the introductory material in the Sacramentary is the *General Instruction of the Roman Missal.* Chapter 2, section 8, tells us:

> Although the Mass is made up of the Liturgy of the Word and the Liturgy of the Eucharist, the two parts are so closely connected as to form one act of worship. The table of God's Word and of Christ's Body is prepared and from it the faithful are instructed and nourished.

The presider, the lector, the commentator, the cantor, and the choir all exercise a ministry of hospitality. The tone of voice, the gestures, and the manner in which they exercise their ministries can show a spirit of hospitality and welcome. In the best exercise of these ministries, they invite worshipers to take the proper roles that are *their* right and duty as part of the baptized and as members of the assembly at a particular liturgy.

A small but beautiful and important way of showing hospitality can be the manner in which the ministers of the Eucharist exercise their ministry. A good host sees to the comfort and service of his or her guests. Jesus, our host at the banquet, has called each of us to roles of service. In many parishes, the ministers of the Eucharist recognize that they have a special role of service to the community. During the singing of the *Lamb of God*, the Eucharistic ministers gather behind the presider either in a large semicircle or in some convenient manner. After the priest-presider has received Communion under both forms, the deacon or another designated assistant or perhaps the presider himself sends two cup ministers and one Communion minister to each station. At two Masses we minister at six stations; at two Masses we minister at four stations; and at two Masses we minister by serving only under the form of bread. Each weekend some sixty people exercise this ministry. In this way, the community itself is exemplified. When the Eucharistic ministers have completed their service role, they reassemble behind the presider. All of the Communion bread is gathered into one container, and the Precious Blood is gathered into two cups. The Eucharistic ministers are then served.

Some parishes offer training sessions for Eucharistic ministers in each season of the year so that there is always an adequate number of people to offer hospitality in this manner. In our parish, over one hundred men and women have gone through the training sessions for Eucharistic ministers.

Following Mass a certain number of these Eucharistic ministers carry their ministry into the parish. In some parishes they are officially sent with a prayer, just before the Communion prayer. Within the boundaries of our parish there are three small hospitals and six nursing homes, which are served each Sunday. In every season there are persons who are homebound as well as certain others who are recuperating from illness. The hospitality of the worshiping community is shared with these people, even as Eucharist was shared with the "absent ones" in the early Church.

4

Sacramental Moments: First Eucharist

Certain sacramental moments call forth special moments of hospitality. One of these moments is the time of the reception of First Eucharist in a family.

As we know, sacraments are not private actions of any one individual, couple, or family. Sacraments are Christ-actions and always involve the entire faith community. Year by year our parish, like every other parish, is involved in preparing our young people to approach the Eucharistic table.

Given the age of the child (six, seven, or eight), he or she will usually want to approach the Eucharistic table because others are called to the Lord's table and have received. Either the child has walked forward as father and mother have approached to receive Eucharist or the child has watched important others, or peers, or perhaps there has been a combination of all three. To "receive Communion" is an important, anticipated moment.

Twice each year we provide opportunities to assist parents, who are the primary educators in the preparation of their children. The word and the example of parents is paramount. They do not always feel adequate to prepare their child without help; therefore, we invite parents to be part of three sessions that explore the theology of Eucharist and the memory of this precious return gift of Jesus to us. Although we continue to work with the child, whether in day school or Sunday school, the parents are aware of the material that the child is working on. They also have a workbook that allows them to assist the child. Although the sacrifice aspect of Eucharist is presented, the meal aspect is also noted. The hospitality of the Lord Jesus in inviting us to the banquet and his participation as host and food-gift are explored.

When the child is deemed ready by the parents, they notify the pastor, the associate pastor, the pastoral assistant, or the director of the religious education program. The parents accompany the child for a special "interview." This sharing session is not really an examination except in the sense of allowing the child to review the stories that have been part of his or her learning experience. The stories of family, the story of the family of Jesus, the stories of Jesus feeding, especially the story of Jesus feeding his apostles at the Last Supper, are shared. This sharing also enables the child, especially if the interview is with one of the priests, to become more at ease with this person, who perhaps has been seen as "distant." During the interview, the "how to" of First Eucharist is explored in a friendly, relaxed atmosphere.

It is in the family group that the child has learned the importance and beauty of Eucharist. On a Sunday the family chooses, the child receives First Eucharist. The family is seated in the front row(s) usually with grandparents, godparents, and friends. They come forward when the *Lamb of God* is being sung and are recognized by the presider. "Today Jane Jones, daughter of Tim and Theresa, is welcomed to the Eucharistic table with her parents and godparents." Beginning before Christmas each year, we have children approaching the Eucharistic table almost every Sunday at an hour that is most suited to that particular family. At the end of the school year, we have a special group celebration of Eucharist for all of the children who have received First Eucharist during the year. At a midafternoon time on that day, a special party with punch and cookies is celebrated in the school cafeteria. In these ways, the parish tries to offer hospitality to a group of little folks who, we hope, will remember and pass on their own stories to their children.

5

Sacramental Moments: First Reconciliation

Another special moment of hospitality is offered to our young people at the second-grade level when they are prepared for the sacrament of reconciliation. The American bishops have written:

> Catechesis for children (in the Sacrament of Reconciliation) must always respect the natural disposition, ability, age and circumstances of individuals. Parents should be involved in the preparation of the children for this sacrament. Catechesis for the Sacrament of Reconciliation is to precede First Communion and must be kept distinct by a clear and unhurried separation. The Sacrament of Reconciliation normally should be celebrated prior to the reception of First Communion.[3]

With this in mind, we offer a program of preparation for this sacramental moment of loving forgiveness and reconciliation.

While the children are being offered material in class during their second-grade year, the parents of these children are invited to be part of three classes that assist parents in the preparation of their children for the sacrament of reconciliation. We discover that many of the parents may have given up on sacramental reconciliation. We discuss with them the teaching of Christ about his forgiveness of sin and sinners. Our Roman Catholic tradition of reconciliation and forgiveness as a sacrament and a means of union in Christ is stressed. We try to help parents share their story by discussing their finest "reconciling" moment and perhaps another that might not have been so fine. Out of their experiences, we try to build a positive approach to this Christ-reconciling moment.

Upon the completion of the classes, we offer an option of three different evenings for which parents can sign up to be present with their child for the celebration of first reconciliation. The music chosen for these evenings is music that both parents and children know. The children are seated at the ends of pews with their parents beside them. In this way the children can join in the dialogue homily that follows the Gospel, which is either proclaimed or told as story. The service follows the format for a celebration of the sacrament of penance with a congregation and individual confession.

On either side of the sanctuary, two chairs are arranged. The parents bring their child forward to be introduced to the priest by name. The parents then retire some distance to give privacy to the confessor and the child. The priest is able to take the child's hand if the child is nervous and listen and speak to the child. He is able to reach out and place his hand on the head or shoulder of the child during the words of sacramental reconciliation. It is a welcoming, hospitable moment.

One of the strongest memories the children carry away is the fact that their parents shared in the celebration of first reconciliation with them. Not only did their parents introduce them to the confessor, but they themselves also approached the confessor for sacramental reconciliation on that occasion.

Given this setting, the child has the opportunity to experience the forgiveness of Christ in an open and happy atmosphere. Celebrating the forgiveness of God is precious to all Christians. The shared hospitality of this moment can be a very powerful, moving, and memorable time.

6

Teaching
(He sat with the two at table and began to teach.)

We Americans are a people on the move. Along with an air base at the edge of the community and a large university, we seem to be a middle-management community. All of these groups make for a time of residence in the community that seldom extends beyond seven or eight years. In our parish each summer, about two hundred families move in and two hundred families move out; therefore, we build our programs and our parish life accordingly.

One of the areas into which we have been able to build parish hospitality is our program called "Basic Catholicism." This is a program of eight sessions. The first is a kind of getting-to-know-you session. The others touch seven basic teachings of the Roman Catholic Church. The name derives from the fact that a lot of Roman Catholics come to the parish and really don't know the "basics." Running through the eight sessions is a strong undercurrent of hospitality. We want those participating to know how important they are to God. We want them to know how important they are to us. We want them to know how important they are to one another. And we want them to know how important they are to our parish and to the entire Church.

Every session has the participants involved in icebreakers to get them (in a sense, *force* them) to meet one another. We discover that Roman Catholics are notoriously bad about reaching out or even greeting one another. So each week there is another icebreaker to get them to learn one another's names. *Do you know me if you don't know my name?* It isn't long before they are finding one another at one of the six Masses on the weekends. For newcomers, this is very special. "I saw someone I knew last week!"

"Basic Catholicism" is offered at the beginning of each season. Originally all eight sessions were taught by the pastor or the associate pastor. Through the years, a team effort has evolved. The pastor teaches two sessions, the pastoral assistant teaches two sessions, and the other four sessions are team taught by couples. This calls these couples to exercise their teaching ministry four times each year and also keeps people from burnout.

As pastor, I try to be around at the beginning of class and at break time of as many of the sessions as possible. This gives me the opportunity to get to know names and faces. I am there to pour coffee or punch, share conversation, answer questions, or just visit.

One target group for "Basic Catholicism" consists of young couples seeking to be married in the Church. For whatever reason, one or perhaps both of the young people may have been away from the active practice of their faith. Even if they are regular in Church attendance, they may not have opened a book, or sat through a class, or seriously discussed their faith with others for years. Another situation presents itself when a person not of the Catholic faith is marrying a Catholic and has no idea what the Catholic Church is all about. In all fairness, that person should be allowed to have some idea of what his or her future partner believes and what will be expected of their children. "Basic Catholicism" is an attempt to respond to this need.

We have any number of people in our faith community who, at whatever age, are just not sure of where the Church is or where the Church is going. Perhaps they woke up one morning and discovered that the Church had passed them by. In *what* is their faith? In *whom* is their faith? We invite these people to be part of "Basic Catholicism" also.

There are still others who have been baptized but not catechized. They know that they are Roman Catholic, and that is about all they know. For whatever reason, they may never have been admitted to First Eucharist. For whatever reason, they may never have been confirmed. Now, at age 25 or 45 or 65 they are asking, "What is it all about?" They are saying, "Help me!"

Another target group for "Basic Catholicism" involves young couples seeking to have a child baptized. All too often, the approaching birth of the child has prompted them to start coming to church. Perhaps they are not attending church at all. They may be asking for baptism for their child, not even knowing why, except that "my mother wants me to do this" or "the baby should be baptized." Many times one or the other of the parents (or future parents) is not Roman Catholic and does not understand Roman Catholic teaching on infant baptism. Perhaps the religious background of the Catholic party is such that he or she is not able to articulate the faith that is in fact deeply felt. Persons like this have the right to know what Roman Catholic Christianity is all about.

Upon the completion of "Basic Catholicism," a special hospitable moment presents itself. There is an interview between the couple and one of the priests in which is reviewed basic information received during the classes. This time with the priest presents an opportunity to discuss what happened in the sessions and to talk about where the couple is in their faith journey. Together we set the date and the time for the baptism of their child. We discuss baptismal godparents and set up a time for them to do a walk-through of the baptismal ceremony.

On the baptismal day the parents and godparents are part

of the entrance procession at Mass. Baptisms are so scheduled that they do not occur every Sunday or at the same Mass time but are spread out through the various weekend Masses. The entire worshiping community is invited to welcome the new little Christian(s) by giving a welcoming sign of applause.

In our parish as in many other parishes, a group of women share in the baptismal ministry by preparing baptismal robes. Beautiful in design but quite simple, they are easily slipped over the head of the child during the ceremony. A baptismal candle is also presented to each infant.

Several years ago a group of young mothers who were very interested in early childhood development got together. They assisted me in preparing a series of follow-up baptismal letters. The letters are sent to the parents every six months until the child is three years old. The content of the letters ties in the physical and psychological development of the child with the religious development that is possible at these various stages of growth and development. They are gentle reminders of what is possible on the part of the parents. We have sessions for three- and four-year-olds as part of our Sunday School of Religion. The biannual letters cease with the invitation to enroll their child in our preschool at age three. At this point, the child's name and the parents' names are turned over to our C.C.E. director. A sample of a baptismal follow-up letter is included at the end of this booklet.

7

Serving
("Let me help—Do, by all means!")

In every parish, persons who are sick and those who are aged are a special area of concern. Their needs, in terms of visits and sacramental ministry, occupy a high priority. As previously mentioned, many of the Eucharistic ministers in our parish visit three small hospitals, several rest homes, and those who are homebound following the Sunday Masses. Through this ministry and other hospital visitations, we discover people who are seriously ill. This allows a ministry to the person who is ill and also a ministry to other members of the family. The people who are ill are remembered at daily and Sunday liturgies. Frequently, other members of the family are contacted for consoling and encouraging visits.

A resurrection ministry has emerged in response to the death of a member of the parish family. Once the hour of the funeral has been arranged, a group of people who have volunteered for various ministries become involved. The organist and cantor are contacted, a group of volunteers from the chancel choir as well as other willing singers are notified. Frequently a funeral service calls together people of many different faiths, Roman Catholics from other parishes, and Catholics from other parts of the state. The volunteer choir acts as a backup group for the sung liturgy that is so important for a funeral service.

When making the funeral arrangements, I explore with the family members the many Scriptural options that are available for them to use at the funeral. I try to discover with them texts and passages that either had meaning for the deceased or have special meaning for the family members in this time of loss. It is from these texts that the funeral homily will be prepared. Christian death is stressed during the funeral homily. Appropriate music for the funeral Mass or service of the Word is chosen.

Due to the small percentage of Roman Catholics in our geographical area, the idea of a wake *service* is uniquely Roman Catholic. I discuss with the family the religious makeup of the group who may attend the wake so that they may make a choice between a scriptural rosary or a Bible service with psalms and hymns. The point is made that the evening service is the appropriate time for a eulogy either by the priest, a family member, or both. Since the wake service is less formal than the funeral Mass, music that might have been personal to the deceased or to the family members can be planned.

Meals sometimes become a problem at a time of a death. The family is asked whether they would like food prepared and brought to the home or whether they would prefer to be served in the Parish Family Center, which seats about fifty people. During the year we fill out "Time and Talent" sheets, and the area of "meals for the bereaved" is noted as a possible service to the parish. Recruits are also solicited through the Women's Organization. From these sources, it has been possible to provide a ministry of hospitality to serve meals for the bereaved as part of our resurrection ministry.

This group of women and men assume several responsibilities. Once the number of people has been ascertained, they plan the meal, prepare the food, set the tables (at the home or in the Parish Family Center), serve the meal, and clear and clean the area when finished. Friendly and comforting words during the meal help to show sympathy and understanding in the name of the parish. The families often seem overwhelmed by the generous sharing that these meals bring. They are always grateful for the donors' list, which is kept and shared with them when the meal is finished.

8

Greeting
("He ran to meet them and bowed low.")

When my parents married in 1914, they moved into what was then a new parish. Our family remained in that parish until the death of my father in 1945. Rarely does this happen in our time. Statistics tell us that American families move as often as every seven years. This poses a problem but also an opportunity for the local parish that would like to extend a hand of Christian hospitality to newcomers.

Sunday by Sunday, either in the Sunday bulletin or during the pulpit announcement or both, we invite newcomers to sign up as members of the parish. We note that there is a stand in the entrance of the church for this purpose. This signing will be followed by a call from the parish secretary welcoming them to the parish. At the same time, she tells them they will be receiving a packet of material that includes a list of parish organizations, a blank census form, a sheet containing information about the parish staff, and some envelopes in order that they may exercise their Christian stewardship. She offers to answer any questions they may have.

Four times each year the social activities committee of the parish council plans a newcomers' evening. It usually takes the form of a wine and cheese party in the Parish Family Center. All of the newcomers whose names have surfaced in the previous quarter are given both written and telephone invitations.

At the newcomers' gathering, representatives from the various parish organizations and from the five parish council commissions make short presentations about the work of each group. A tour of the parish school, which includes the gym and cafeteria, is conducted. The newcomers are also given a tour of the rectory.

Each year the social activities committee sponsors general parish get-togethers. These are social activities, not fundraisers. Again, a special effort is made to invite newcomers to be part of such evenings. At one particular gathering, newcomers are given special recognition. They, in turn, are invited to take a role in offering hospitality, even as it has been extended to them.

9

Day by Day
(To see thee more clearly)

The early morning daily Mass is not offered in the cathedral. We have some gathering space in our Parish Family Center, and it becomes worship space at 6:55 A.M., Monday through Friday. On an average, twenty-five to thirty people are present to offer Eucharist. Through most of the year it is the same group, and they are on a first-name basis. After a few years, they all know one another's foibles. ("Did you notice John always clears his throat just before Monsignor begins the homily?" "Who was the new person sitting in the back row?") The stranger or the out-of-towner in our midst can easily be recognized. They get a special welcome after Mass.

At the exit of the worship space, there is a counter area where people can pick up a cup of hot tea or coffee on the way to work or home. A group of people remain after Mass to pray morning prayer together. The number varies from four to fifteen, depending on the day and the season. While I am unvesting, the group prepares the prayer books. One person is putting muffins in the oven. The six-week muffin recipe usually does not last beyond six days! By the time we finish morning prayer, we are ready for some kind of fresh fruit ("I'll bring some fresh peaches, our tree is loaded!") followed by the muffins and hot coffee or tea. Some must rush off to various tasks, but others remain to enjoy time together. All of the early morning Mass group know they are welcome to remain.

During the day, the coffee bar area gets a real workout. Members of the cathedral staff catch their coffee breaks there, and so do the postman and any salespersons who visit with any regularity. People who come for interviews of whatever kind are also welcomed with this ongoing hospitality.

Conclusion

The Official Catholic Directory, which is published every year by the Kenedy Company, contains a lot of numbers and also the names of many places and people. From this book you get a picture of the organization that is the Roman Catholic Church in the United States. But it is all on paper. It can seem remote and cold when reduced to statistics in a book. This is why our parish church and the people who make up our parish are so important. The parish is where Church happens. All of us together try not only to make the message and deeds of Christ come alive but, through worship and day-to-day living and interacting, to make Christ continue to be present to ourselves and to one another.

The graciousness of Christian hospitality underlines and flows through the many ministries that have emerged at worship in our time. Christian hospitality flows out of the good news that Christ is in you and that Christ is in me. It seems that, in every age, individual Christians must rediscover this truth for themselves. It is a basic truth, yet we continue to wrestle with it. Once grasped, it forever changes us. Once grasped, it leads us to a loving service that offers and *provides* a sustaining environment, where we know we are at home with self and others. Hospitality brings a Christ-like charm and delight to every ministry in which we serve and every action that we perform.

References

1. John L. McKenzie, "Hospitality," *Dictionary of the Bible* (New York: Macmillan, 1965) 374.

2. *The Harvard Classics, Folk-Lore and Fable* (New York: Collier and Son, 1909) 17:22.

3. *National Catechetical Directory for Catholics of the United States*, "Sharing the Light of Faith," Sec. 126, "Catechesis of Children for Reconciliation" (Department of Education, USCC, Washington, D.C., 1979).

Booklets on the various ministries are available from The Liturgical Press. Especially helpful is *The Ministry of Evangelization*, which has a fine section on hospitality in a parish.

Litany of Hospitality

Rabbi, there are some lepers here.
    Let them come unto me
Go away children, don't bother the Master.
    Let them come unto me
Lord, you are tired, the crowds must be told to go away.
    Let them come unto me
But Lord, they are blind and crippled.
    Let them come unto me
Lord, they are hungry and poor.
    Let them come unto me
This woman was caught in adultery!
    Let them come unto me
Even sinners and thieves?
    Let them come unto me
They are man, woman and child.
    Let them come unto me.

—Dena Gonzales

Examination of Conscience for a Member of the Assembly

Am I a welcoming person?
Is there room in my life for others or am I too busy?
Do I extend the welcoming gesture, the warm smile?
Do I hear with my heart as well as with my head?
Do I go out of my way even when it is not convenient to do so?
Do I try to use inclusive language whenever possible?
As a liturgical minister, do I function as a member of the team?
Do I work on my own spiritual development?
Am I open to full, conscious participation at worship and in parish activities?
Do I make an effort to encounter Jesus Christ in the people with whom I work and worship?
Am I a promoter of social justice?

—Sherry Bitsche

Baptismal Follow-up Letter
(First letter in a series of four)

(date)

Mr. and Mrs. John Doe
2222 St. Joe Street
Lubbock, TX 79413

Dear Mr. and Mrs. Doe,

A few months ago the Cathedral of Christ the King celebrated with you the baptism of Christopher. As he was welcomed into our faith-community, all of us promised to support you in nurturing his new life as a child of God. This letter is intended as a word of support from us to you.

Crib toys, rattles, pictures, and perhaps mobiles have by now been given to your child by yourselves, your relatives and friends to dazzle his opening eyes and ears with the beauty of the sights and sounds of our wonderful world. The baptismal liturgy we celebrated with you used very ordinary elements, fire, water and oil, to awaken your child to the Creator-Father who said all of His Creation was "very good" (Gen 1:31). This is a very sensual time in the growth of your child, and the fire, water, and oil addressed those awakening senses with the Good News of God's Life in the world about.

May we suggest that, if you haven't already done this, you place some visual faith-image (a cross, statue, or holy picture) in the child's environment and periodically draw his attention to it. (These items can be ordered through the parish office.) It is not too early to begin your faith-sharing with him as you (and we) promised in the baptismal rite.

We join with you in prayer and effort for the continued growth in faith of your child. If there is anything we can do to help, don't hesitate to call. Meanwhile, see you in church!

Sincerely in Christ,